Redemptive Poverty Work

Mentor's Guide

Redemptive Poverty Work Mentor's Guide

© 2023. The Urban Ministry Institute. All Rights Reserved.

Copying, redistribution, and/or sale of these materials, or any unauthorized transmission, except as may be expressly permitted by the 1976 Copyright Act or in writing from the publisher is prohibited. Requests for permission should be addressed in writing to:

The Urban Ministry Institute
3701 East 13th Street North
Suite 100
Wichita, KS 67208

ISBN: 978-1-62932-059-5

Published by TUMI Press
A division of World Impact, Inc.

The Urban Ministry Institute is a ministry of World Impact, Inc.

All Scripture quotations, unless otherwise noted, are from The Holy Bible, English Standard Version, copyright © 2001 by Crossway Bible. A division of Good News Publishers. Used by permission. All Rights Reserved.

REDEMPTIVE POVERTY WORK

Alvin Sanders

Mentor's Guide

TUMI Press
3701 East 13th Street North
Suite 100
Wichita, Kansas 67208

Table of Contents

7	Redemptive Poverty Work Course Introduction
11	**Lesson 1** A Brief Theological Reflection
17	**Lesson 2** Toxic Poverty Work
23	**Lesson 3** Redemptive Poverty Work
31	**Lesson 4** Rhythms of Life and Poverty Work

Appendix

41	Appendix 1: Course Schedule for *Redemptive Poverty Work*
45	Appendix 2: *Redemptive Poverty Work* Course Survey

Redemptive Poverty Work
Course Introduction

Your first session will be an orientation. This is part of the class requirements for the students, and attendance is mandatory. In this session you will provide the expectations of the class, the grading policy, when assignments are due, and how quizzes will be administered, etc. If this is an online course using World Impact U (WIU), you will also orient the students to WIU, how to answer forum questions, and how to submit assignments.

There are also two videos to show the class during this session:

- *An Opportunity to Learn Redemptive Poverty,* Dr. Don Davis
- *The Dirty Little Secret of Poverty Work*, Dr. Alvin Sanders

Here are some suggestions as to what to cover in this first session:

Welcome

1. Open in prayer.
2. Provide your full name and Email address so that the students know how to reach you.
3. Remind the students that they should already have copies of the books:
   - *Redemptive Poverty Work*, Dr. Alvin Sanders
   - *Uncommon Church: Community Transformation for the Common Good*, Dr. Alvin Sanders
4. Allow students to introduce themselves, their ministry, and what they hope to get out of the class.

Introduction

Video: Watch the video *An Opportunity to Learn Redemptive Poverty,* by Dr. Don Davis, on how we need a clear, biblical, and compelling perspective on what it means to conduct life-affirming care in communities of poverty.

Introduce **Redemptive Poverty Work** *Concept*

1. *Redemptive Poverty Work* was developed from reviewing a "Redemptive Frame" and applying it to World Impact. A Redemptive Frame states

that there are three ways you work throughout the world: Exploitatively, Ethically, and Redemptively. You then take this frame and put it on top of your non-profit and the work that you do. Since World Impact does poverty work, working with people in communities of poverty, we have *Redemptive Poverty Work* (RPW).

2. Christianity was birthed out of people who lived in conditions of poverty, and to this day the overwhelming majority of people who ascribe to Christianity live in the condition of poverty. So it's very important to understand what Christ's view of the condition of poverty was and how he expected us to minister in it.

3. Now that we have RPW, World Impact has discovered that this is not only going to help the people with whom we already minister, but it is also opening doors to totally new audiences who would have never listened to us or even saw the reason to listen to us before.

4. Here are some examples:

   - There is a group of energy providers in the Atlanta, Georgia, area where we had connections with them previously. When Dr. Sanders presented RPW to this secular audience they loved it. So much so, that several CEOs of Public Utility Companies have reached out to see how they can partner with World Impact.

   - Dr. Sanders did a pilot training of RPW for two of the largest churches in Louisville, Kentucky, and they loved it because they discovered they had been doing a lot of toxic poverty work.

   - A missions pastor of a large church with several satellite churches said that RPW is how he could share the heart of service at his church.

5. This is for anybody and everybody who's interested in following the model of Jesus Christ and working with people who are in poverty, whether you're in poverty now or have never been in poverty. The only thing you need is an interest in working in communities of poverty as Christ worked in communities of poverty. It could be

a donor, an inner city pastor, a volunteer worker at a food pantry, a teacher, etc.

6. The mindset that we are developing for redemptive poverty work is to be able to look and act as Jesus did with us of creative restoration through sacrifice. For the people we are working with, we want to be able to provide pathways of opportunity, and to help them to understand that they can be used by God and to exist within the condition that they find themselves. Some may choose to try to better themselves and others may never get out of the situation they are in. What we can't forget is regardless of their material possessions, God loves them, and God is with them to use them.

7. The goal of this course is to have a practical theology of how to do successful redemptive poverty work.

Course Description and Syllabus

Review Course Description, Objectives, and Syllabus (found on pages 9-12 of the Student Workbook).

The following are some key points to make about each lesson:

- Lesson 1: *A Brief Theological Reflection*

    This lesson is not meant to be a thorough insight of everything the Bible has to say about people in poverty and the condition of poverty. Instead, if asked why are we doing this, you will have a practical theological answer.

- Lesson 2: *Toxic Poverty Work*

    In this lesson, we talk about the problem of toxic poverty work, which comes directly from an exploitative mindset.

    We will discuss how this can be an unconscious mindset, and that good intentions are not enough. Each person must engage their moral attitudes and mindset as to why they are doing poverty work and ask, "Is it biblical?"

- Lesson 3: *Redemptive Poverty Work*

  In this lesson we define exactly what redemptive poverty work is, what it is about, and how it differs from toxic poverty work.

- Lesson 4: *Rhythms of Life and Poverty Work*

  Our final lesson shows how we can use eight spiritual disciplines to enhance our walk as a believer in Jesus Christ and prevent burnout.

Forum and Forms

Ensure students have access to the forum and to the forms they will need to complete their assignments. (These forms can be found online on the WIU Redemptive Poverty Work Dashboard.)

- Assignment Checklist
- Reading Completion Sheet
- Scripture Memory Grading Form
- Class Schedule with Assignments and Due Dates

Review the forms, forum use, and course requirements with the students.

Introduction to Redemptive Poverty Work

As a final step in this class session, watch *The Dirty Little Secret of Poverty Work*. which gives an overview of the three major approaches to serving individuals and families in at-risk communities, i.e., Exploitative, Ethical, and Redemptive, and lays the foundation for your entire training. Understanding the principles and practice of redemptive poverty work is essential for all those seeking justice and peace in communities of poverty.

Remind the students of their next class meeting and any assignments that need to be completed before the Lesson 1 class meeting.

A Brief Theological Reflection

MENTOR'S NOTES 1

📖 **1**
page 13
Lesson Introduction

Welcome to the Mentor's Guide for *Redemptive Poverty Work*, Lesson 1: *A Brief Theological Reflection*. This lesson provides a simple practical theology for poverty work. Specifically, this lesson emphasizes three biblical themes that undergird why we do what we do. As you lead your students through these biblical themes, make sure to give ample time to the Scriptures themselves. Students should understand clearly that Redemptive Poverty Work is rooted in Scripture. Help them to engage the Old Testament principles of empowerment and to truly consider Jesus's own favor for the poor and warnings against riches.

Christians are much more likely than non-Christians to view poverty as the result of personal failure. This mentality leads to the poverty-stricken being treated as "projects" instead of people to serve, which is not what God intended. It is the aim of this lesson to provide a biblical corrective to these attitudes and assumptions. The Bible gives significant instruction concerning how we are to treat those in poverty. Throughout this lesson, and the lessons to come, keep Scripture central for your students.

📖 **2**
page 16
Summary

Emphasize the importance of biblical literacy.

1. There's been a complete flipping of people's ability to engage Scripture and apply it, and a heavy emphasis on advocacy and advocacy alone being the answer as to what ails people who live in the condition of poverty.

2. We should not try to divorce the two:
   - Believe in evangelism AND justice.
   - Believe in individual sin and systemic institutional sin.

3. We want to be champions and conveyors of that theological truth.

4. Biblical illiteracy is at an all-time high within our pews. Even for common biblical stories like Noah and the ark or Joseph and his brothers, half of those in church would not know about these. Don't assume that people know the Bible. If people don't generally know the Bible, then they definitely don't know what it says about poverty or the condition of poverty.

📖 3
page 16
Outline Point I

I. Poverty Is a Theme in Both the Old and New Testaments

The following are key insights to note as you discuss this section with your students.

1. The Bible is a book of the working poor.

2. Poverty is a lack of financial resources for people to be able to take care of the needs that they have in their life.

3. The Bible gives us many reasons for a lack of these resources.

   - Personal sin – example is the prodigal son. He had plenty of money but blew it all because of his attitude and character.

   - Societal/Institutional sin – people are in poverty simply because of the society that they live in; things that society does to keep certain groups of people in poverty and liberate others financially.

4. It's not either/or; it could be both/and.

5. In the USA, statistically most people in poverty were born into it and most of them don't switch poverty classes. (NOTE: This may be different in your country.)

6. The working poor is a theme that is woven throughout the Bible. The focus was not on how people got into that condition, but rather how can we create pathways of opportunity.

📖 4
page 16
Outline Point A

A. Old Testament Principles of Empowerment

Help your students understand the following:

1. The Old Testament focused on creating pathways of opportunity.

2. The Bible is not necessarily focused on causation. The Old Testament focused on creating pathways of opportunity for people to be able to survive their condition or transcend their condition

and understand that God is bigger than the circumstances they find themselves in.

- An example of this is a church that provided full tuition scholarships for God-loving kids in poverty, who had the potential and interest of going to college, but not the opportunity. With getting a college degree, they have become productive members of society and are no longer in poverty.

3. The Bible could have been situated in the condition of poverty to begin with because in almost every culture, you are looked down upon if you don't have enough resources (a second-class citizen).

- In the Bible, the nation of Israel wasn't looked at as a powerful nation, but a ragtag group of people who were in slavery. But God said they, the underdog, were going to be his people. The whole point of the book of Exodus is that God delivered them out of Egypt.

- Also, there were other people/nations in Egypt, and when they saw what the God of the Israelites did, they went with the Israelites. They saw what God did to the "mighty" Egyptian nation and how God humbled the Egyptian god.

B. Jesus Favored the Poor / C. Jesus Warned against Riches

page 17
Outline Points B and C

Highlight the following about these two outline points:

1. Jesus and most biblical characters were the working poor.

2. Jesus chose to live in a working poor situation.

3. Jesus was making a very big statement by showing that you need to value people in poverty.

4. Jesus chose to be a rabbi who didn't have a lot of prestige and didn't command a lot of earthly power. He did so as a model of humility.

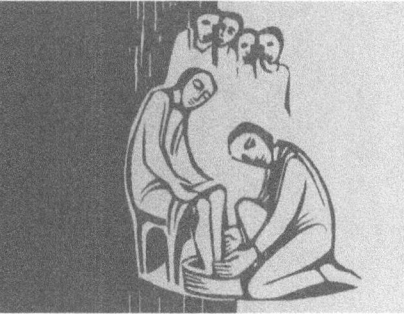

5. God can transcend wherever you are as a person, or as a church, as in the Book of Acts.

6. Empowerment is more important than causation.

    - Focus on creating pathways of opportunity.

    - For people who live in the condition of poverty, know that is not their identity, but the condition that they live in.

    - We should respect their talents and abilities and understand that God will utilize them.

page 19
Student Questions and Response

Now allow the students to comment on what was presented. Here are some topics that can be discussed if you need to get the discussion going. (NOTE: Don't feel obligated to use them. If your class is going along well, allow the students to discuss freely.)

- World Impact provides effective, affordable, and accessible seminary programs which is a pathway of opportunity. This is directly from the Scriptures.

- The number one reason that pastors don't have formal training is they don't have the money.

- A non-faith-based organization can take some of the principles of redemptive poverty work and do good things; they can make the world a better place. A part of redemptive poverty work is ethical poverty work.

- Discuss working poor in ministry. God has created each of us for a purpose and given us gifts and talents to be able to go out and make the world a better place. So, if we go forth and try to do what we were created to do and expand the Kingdom, there will be provision made for us to have enough.

- Genesis 3 makes it very clear that we live in a fallen world, therefore you will experience hardship in your life. God will utilize those hardships when we engage with others. God will turn your test into a testimony. Trust in God's promises that everything will be all right eventually, even though you may not see it in YOUR lifetime.

- Most people never emerge from poverty.

- The number-one reason why people are in poverty is that they were born into it.

- Or use the following for in-class discussion:

    1. Why are people biblically illiterate?

    2. Besides it being a kingdom priority, what are your top three reasons for pursuing poverty work from a biblical perspective?

    3. Are there legitimate reasons to not pursue it?

📖 7
page 20
Case Study

Discuss the Case Study:

A young urban minister who oversees training volunteers for a tutoring program for a school in an impoverished neighborhood has come to you for advice. Her job is to give an orientation before the volunteers are assigned kids to work with. She has found that she consistently runs into a problem. Every orientation a debate breaks out among the new volunteers concerning the causes of poverty. One group argues that people are poor because they made bad choices in their lives. The others argue that people are poor because of economic injustice. Rarely does either group cite Scripture to back up their arguments. What is your advice to her?

- After some have provided their input, let them know that it does add value to know their backgrounds so we can be informative.

- If you engage people theologically from what the Bible says about poverty, you will address the volunteer's concern.

- Create a pathway of opportunity, regardless of how they got there – love them as God has commanded us to love them, empower them to make their situations better if they desire, and empower them to do that by creative restoration through sacrifice.

Toxic Poverty Work

MENTOR'S NOTES 2

📖 **1**
page 23
Lesson Introduction

Welcome to the Mentor's Guide for *Redemptive Poverty Work*, Lesson 2: *Toxic Poverty Work*. This lesson outlines the type of poverty work that naturally arises from our sinful nature. Take some time to clarify this theological point. As image-bearers of Almighty God and followers of Christ, we often seek to do good for those in poverty. However, if we follow our natural impulses with unreflective acts of "service" we often produce *Toxic Poverty Work*. The care and concern of God for the poor can be twisted in ways that are self-serving and destructive.

With this framework in mind, survey the toxic forms our work can take if we do not practice self-awareness. Much of this lesson will recall experiences for your students. You may have people who have done *Toxic Poverty Work* and people who have been the recipients of such work. Allow your students to share and discuss their own experiences of savior syndrome, paternalism, burnout, and cynicism. Healthy poverty work begins when we grapple with the foundational weakness built into our work – the idealistic belief that we can rescue people from their circumstances.

📖 **2**
page 26
Summary

Mindset leads to behaviors, and behaviors affect goals.

1. We come to a situation with certain values, attitudes, and beliefs about said situation or person (our mindset).

2. That will lead to certain behaviors which then affects our goals.

3. For example, an exploitative mindset can lead to toxic behaviors.

4. Genesis 3 tells us that we all sin and fall short of the glory of God. Because of that, if we don't disrupt our thought processes, we're going to do things that may be good coming from our natural selves, but other things we will try to do for selfish reasons.

   📖 3
page 26
Outline Point I

I. Savior Syndrome: Taking on a Role God Never Intended Us to Have

1. We want to go in, save and rescue people and their communities.

2. None of us have the ability to save anybody. We can't save ourselves. We can be used by God to be able to make situations better.

3. We don't have stated intentions to exploit people in poverty, nor do we want to go into a neighborhood and be toxic.

4. Having it brought to your attention that you are not supposed to go out and rescue people, but you're still out there trying to rescue people.

5. If we don't address our ability or our presupposition to go and try to save people, we will end up with a lot of heartache, pain, and suffering. The only thing that people need from us is that Jesus is within us.

   📖 4
page 27
Outline Point II

II. Paternalism: An Issue of Power Dynamics

1. In offering help, we feel like we are the parent and those in poverty are the child and therefore can't take care of themselves and don't have a voice to engage or give input into their own dreams, hopes, goals, etc.

2. We assume we know what's best.

3. Don't be a dictator. Don't come in, take over, and dictate what is to be done and how it should be done. If we do know what's best, then we should work alongside the individual or the community to find the best way forward with their input and build things together.

III. Burnout and Cynicism: Suffering from Fatigue and Disillusionment

📖 5
page 27
Outline Point III

Burnout: Suffering from Fatigue

1. Comprised of three things:

    - Having the wrong mindset

    - Continuing to try to save people from their situation

    - Trying to control things all the time (paternalism)

2. Analogous to going 100 miles/hour and not taking care of yourself.

3. A healthy dose of reality that not everything will work out can prevent burnout. We think that what we are doing is going to be miraculous in this community, and when it doesn't happen, it can lead to burnout.

4. We need to take time to reenergize and not be available 24/7. If we are available all the time, something's wrong.

5. Burnout can cause people to leave the church, to question their faith and walk away from the Lord.

Cynicism: Suffering from Disillusionment

1. Essentially, cynicism is when we lose hope. We may feel big doing the work of ministry, but we are cynical about everything and everyone around us; we think that there's no hope for the people or neighborhoods in poverty. Really, we have become heartbroken.

2. It is the cousin of burnout.

3. Everything seems horrible and terrible, like there's no good in the world or in people.

4. Every cynic used to be an idealist.

5. Poverty work can spur us to be cynics because there is so much complexity that we are engaging in when we're dealing with people, especially with those in the condition of poverty.

📖 **6**
page 29
Conclusion

In summary, we've had the wrong mindset when we've gone into situations which led to toxic behaviors which has then led to the wrong goals.

📖 **7**
page 29
Student Questions and Response

Now allow the students to comment on what was presented. Here are some topics that can be discussed if you need to get the discussion going. (NOTE: Don't feel obligated to use them. If your class is going along well, allow the students to discuss freely.)

- There may be some people who are ready to receive the truth. With others you simply walk away. Don't argue with them. People typically fall into one of two camps:

    1. Those who want to pretend like they understand, and they want to argue with you all day long.

    2. Those who are trying to figure things out and you can engage (interact with) them.

- When we help someone and they give their life to Christ, that is just the beginning. We should be prepared with a system or have a strategy in place so that when someone gives their life to Christ, we know the steps that will help us invest in and encourage them to grow in their faith.

- We should try to model what Jesus did for us in the Scriptures. When Jesus met people at their point of need, he let them know what his motivation was.

- Or use the following discussion questions:

    1. Have you ever lived in poverty? How does your experience (or lack of it) affect your understanding of poverty?

    2. How easy or hard is it for you to accept that if you have participated in poverty work, at some point, you have practiced toxic poverty work?

    3. What issues do you need to personally engage in after learning of toxic poverty work?

📖 **8**
page 30
Case Study

Discuss the Case Study:

Some friends ask you to visit the Christian food pantry they volunteer at. As someone they trust, they want you to observe and give your opinion on its operations. The first thing you notice as you walk up are some shirtless guys gambling, smoking, and drinking right around the entrance. When you walk in, you are struck by how dark and dingy the interior is. Things seem chaotic and you cannot discern any rhyme or reason to how people receive their groceries. People are getting antsy waiting. Then a young preacher comes into the waiting area and gives a sermon. When he is done, everyone raises their hand to receive Christ. After about an hour, the first person goes forward to get a bag of groceries, which turns into a huge argument between the volunteer and the customer over food choices. The volunteer tells him that he gets whatever is given to him, and he should be happy about it. Afterwards, you go out to lunch with your friends to discuss your observations. What do you tell them?

Let the students respond to this, but here are some suggested items to start off with:

1. I would go deeper in my observation, into the program itself. What is the intention of the program? Why did they start it?

2. What is toxic about this situation:

    - Front door environment

    - Those serving (training needed)

    - Esthetics

    - Holding people hostage

    - Disorganized – the way it is set up creates a lot of problems, instead of bringing solutions or making people feel comfortable when receiving the food.

    - Shows that the people coming for help are not being valued.

3. It's important that the people who are being served have ownership. They should believe that what you are doing/providing really benefits them.

4. We should provide assistance with the thought of sustainability. Offer assistance at the request of and alongside the people who are going to be in a community long term, strengthening the program and the calling that God has put on their lives and hearts. That's what will bring lasting change.

Redemptive Poverty Work

📖 **1**
page 33
Lesson Introduction

Welcome to the Mentor's Guide for *Redemptive Poverty Work*, Lesson 3: *Redemptive Poverty Work*. This lesson defines the goal of our activity by exploring the three types of poverty work available to us. The first of the three types, the *Exploitative Mindset*, builds directly on the previous discussion of toxic poverty work. In some ways, the exploitative mindset is ignoring the potential for toxicity in poverty work. Help your students make this connection and show them how toxic poverty work and the exploitative mindset go hand-in-hand.

The second mindset, the *Ethical Mindset*, acknowledges the good that anyone can do in society. Not every action of poverty workers will be toxic or have destructive consequences. Even apart from a redemptive model, people often work for the common good in ethical ways. Help your students to think of organizations and people that do ethical poverty work. Such organizations and people can be legitimate and helpful partners for us as we do redemptive poverty work.

The third mindset, *Redemptive Poverty Work*, imitates the work that Christ has done on the cross as we pursue redemption of lives and neighborhoods. It is crucial that your students see the connection between Christ's own redemptive work and the work we seek to do. *Redemptive Poverty Work* is not a new strategy or an innovative idea. It is simply modeling our poverty work after Christ's own self-sacrificial redemptive work. There can be no more reliable methodology than what God has employed in Christ.

📖 2
page 36
Outline Point I

I. Three Distinct Mindsets When It Comes to How We Approach Poverty Work

There are three types of work that happens within the world that you read about or saw in the video.

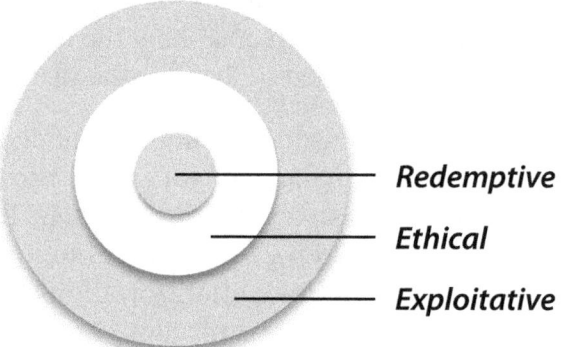

A. The outer layer of our self-awareness is the *Exploitative Mindset* of Poverty Work.

1. Leads to the savior syndrome mentality

2. I am here to rescue you and your neighborhood.

3. It's all about me.

4. It's not intentional, but it happens because we're not conscious of ourselves and how we're moving in a particular person's life or in a particular community.

5. You're trying to get something out of someone or out of a community.

6. The question becomes, "Do we ever mature and realize that I am not here for me, that I am here to represent God? The people in this community don't need me, they need the Jesus in me. They need to know the Good News."

B. The next level up in our self-awareness is the *Ethical Mindset* of Poverty Work.

1. This is the highest level one can achieve without knowing Christ.

2. Nothing wrong with ethical poverty work

3. You have evolved beyond; from "I am here for me" to "I'm actually here for these people."

4. It's a win-win mentality. "I want to win, you want to win, so let's work together and collaborate so that everyone wins in this situation."

5. Ethical Poverty Work is the foundation of what God is calling World Impact to do, which is Redemptive Poverty Work.

C. Finally, there is the *Redemptive Mindset* of Poverty Work.

1. Creative restoration through sacrifice

2. It has everything to do with motive and the rate of restoration through sacrifice. It's following the pattern that Christ followed to redeem us.

3. Motivated to sacrifice our time and treasures because Christ did the same for us

4. We are not the savior of this community (we are working in) but Christ is the Savior. We want to introduce them to the ways of Christ so that they may be able to take a pathway of opportunity when it comes to them being in poverty.

📖 3
page 37
Outline Point II

II. Redemptive Work in the Bible

Characteristics of Redemptive Poverty Work:

- Ethical empowerment
- Creative restoration through sacrifice
- God is bigger than the circumstances.
- Poverty is a condition, not an identity.
- Walk by faith while rearranging human systemic power.

1. Ethical empowerment

    - I sacrifice, you win. It matters how we do things. It matters how people respond.
    - It's not just about us, it's not just about them, it's about working together collaboratively so that God can receive and get all the glory.

2. Creative restoration through sacrifice

    - The pattern that Christ used to redeem us.
    - Because of what Jesus has done for us, we want to do so for others.
    - You are doing this and trying to work to make the situation better for people who live in a condition of poverty whether it benefits you or not. You are going to sacrifice and try to make their lives better, just like what Christ has done for the entire world.

3. God is bigger than the circumstances.

    - This is obvious but easily forgettable.
    - God is bigger than the circumstances that we see, and God is big in spite of the circumstances.

- When we look at situations – people's lives and neighborhoods – we always have faith that God can overcome this and that God can use me to make a difference in that situation.

Our Role as Redemptive Poverty Workers

page 37
Outline Point III

Poverty is a condition, not an identity.

1. The big mistake of society is that our social class standing becomes our identity. It has a big influence on us.

2. We should engage that, and not allow our social status to become ALL of our identity.

3. Especially for those in poverty, their existence from a societal standpoint is put on a lower level of humanity because they don't have a lot of financial resources. Most do not want to live in their neighborhood.

4. God uses people whether we are wealthy, or have no money at all, or are somewhere in between.

5. And as a side note – racial identity is tied up in all of this as well. You may not know where race begins, and social class ends. They really don't. They are tied up in one big ball together, so that if you are black or brown, it's assumed that you're poor or live in poverty or know about poverty.

6. Our proper lens is to view people in poverty the same way we would view anybody else and not assign negative connotations to them. God has given them the same gifting and talents he has given everybody else. The Kingdom of God is moving amongst them through the power of the local church.

7. In Ephesians, the Apostle Paul understood that his identity was not in whatever condition he found himself in, but that his identity was always in being a child of God and follower of Jesus Christ.

8. Because Christ is with us, that is what we put our faith, hope, and trust in.

Walk by faith while rearranging human systemic power.

1. Our advocacy and going into social justice situations are with the eye of God. We want God to move in these situations.

2. We are motivated by theological principles. Social and cultural principles enhance those theological principles. You can tie in the social and the cultural landscape after the theological foundation has been laid.

3. When we engage those forces that are trying to make people less than human and trying to make communities less than what their true potential is . . . we know that what we're doing is by faith in God. Regardless of the outcome, it does not change the fact that we are always striving to make this world a better place.

📖 5
page 38
Student Questions and Response

Now allow the students to comment on what was presented. Here are some topics that can be discussed if you need to get the discussion going. (NOTE: Don't feel obligated to use them. If your class is going along well, allow the students to discuss freely.)

- The Church needs to define where it fits in with the social upheavals and shifting. When it comes to social issues taking place all over the world, oftentimes, the Church is very silent. They don't want to get involved in political matters or believe these are political matters and should not be engaged by the Church.

- Because the churches are silent, many young people are looking for places and spaces where they can find advocacy.

- Is it possible for a church to work alongside an organization that is not ethical or exploits people if it's for the common good?

- Lead with the Word and then tell the truth about social conditions that exist.

- On an institutional level, confront injustice. On a personal level, the Bible tells us to create pathways of opportunity for people who are in the condition of poverty to live a more humane life and to switch social classes. But some/many may not switch social classes. It is important to know that Jesus is with us even in the midst of our suffering.

- Or use the following discussion questions:

    1. How has redemption changed your personal life?

    2. Does the notion of redemptive poverty work resonate with you? Explain why or why not.

    3. What is the main difference between *ethical* and *redemptive* poverty work?

📖 6
page 39
Case Study

Discuss the Case Study:

You have been working with Sheri for five years. By all accounts, Sheri is a good woman with a rock-solid faith. She attends church every Sunday that she is not scheduled to work at a hotel as a maid. She brings home just enough money to make ends meet for her and her three children, as their father does not contribute much to their lives. Right now, she is upset because she just found out that one of her sons has been expelled from a private Christian school that you played a key role in getting him admitted to. On one hand, she is embarrassed; on the other, she feels invisible to God because in her opinion the school is over-reacting because of his race and social class. What is your response to her?

Let the students respond to this, but here are some suggested items to start off with:

- Since I took part in getting the young man in the school, I would feel a responsibility to talk to the administration to hear their side of the story and then hear from the young man.

- Since it states in the case study that the father doesn't play a part in the kids' life, I would see if there is a man in the church that could be a mentor to him. He could use some solid biblical male guidance.

- At the end of the discussion, explain the reason for the expulsion and see if that changes anyone's opinion: The young man wore one of his older brother's T-shirts that had a marijuana leaf on it. From the culture in which he grew up in, there was nothing to it. He wasn't doing or selling drugs. The school felt it was aggressive and instead of talking it out to see what could be learned from a cultural perspective from both sides, they stated that they don't advocate drugs and ruled his behavior sinful and wrong and expelled him. The school is killing a fly with a sledgehammer.

Rhythms of Life and Poverty Work

 1
page 43
Lesson Introduction

Welcome to the Mentor's Guide for *Redemptive Poverty Work*, Lesson 4: *Rhythms of Life and Poverty Work*. This lesson lays out spiritual practices for poverty work that are connected to the Great Tradition of the Church.

It is essential that you help your students understand what is meant by *The Great Tradition*. Here is a good working definition: "The Great Tradition represents the central core of Christian belief and practice derived from Scripture that runs between the time of Christ and the middle of the fifth century" (Dr. Don Davis, *Sacred Roots*, TUMI: 2010, p. 74).

Here is a helpful expansion on this definition: "It is the legacy of early Christian engagement with Scripture that fundamentally shaped the Church as we know it. The early church built a rule of faith (a creed) that summarizes the core of the faith from Scripture. They created a service of the Word and the Table that keys all gathered worship to the Gospel of Christ and his Kingdom. They Christianized the Jewish festival calendar to pattern their own spiritual lives on the story of God in Christ. The Word of God dwelt richly in them and they became a light representing Christ and his Kingdom in the world. Their beliefs and practices became the Sacred Roots of every branch of the church" (Ryan Carter, *Guard the Good Deposit*, TUMI: 2019, pp. 11-12).

Poverty work has been essential to the Church from her earliest days. The Great Tradition developed not apart from poverty but in the midst of it. In fact, many early Christians were from the poor, low, and despised classes of society. The contention of this lesson is that Redemptive Poverty Work cannot be separated from the beliefs and practices of Great Tradition. It is critical that you help your students maintain the proper link in their mind between who we are as the Church and what we do in the world. If we truly hope to see people and neighborhoods redeemed, our work must flow from and build to a robust church life rooted in the Great Tradition.

The spiritual practices outlined in this lesson are designed to help you and your students embrace and embody in this conviction. They are practical ways for us to enact our shared life, shared journey, shared discipline and shared confession.

📖 2
page 45
Summary

In working in communities of poverty and serving those whose lives are being taxed by spiritual, physical, or psychological trauma, it's going to be a challenge to maintain the freshness and strength that you need. You can get that freshness and strength from these Rhythms of Life. They can safeguard us from being burned out, being toxic ourselves, and from being overly stressed.

Three months living and working in communities that are stressed and economically deprived and socially under the gun is enough to break all altruism that you started with.

People called to serve in these communities often think that because God has called them to poverty work, they will be fine. What they discover is that their own personal lives, their minds, their bodies, the lack of sleep, the long hours, all the things that come with ministering in these communities are affected. They find that they themselves are the object of the devil's attack.

You can't give to others what you do not personally own. "You can't give what you ain't got, and you can't lose what you ain't never had" (Muddy Waters). So the first thing above everything else in doing ministry in at-risk neighborhoods is your own soul care.

📖 3
page 47
Outline Point B, 1

Church Membership

- Commit to active membership within a healthy local church for the purposes of fellowship, teaching, prayer, service, and personal development.

- Being a part of a church community allows you to receive pastoral care, good feeding/teaching, fellowship, and blessings.

- It is critical to *Redemptive Poverty Work* because the main redemptive institution for the world, that we see from the Bible's teachings, is the local church.

- The church is a vibrant institution that is supposed to be the group of people who have been called to redeem the world to do the things that they need to keep themselves connected to God.

📖 4
page 48
Outline Point B, 2

Fixed Times of Prayer

- Prayer allows us to stop seeing circumstances as bigger than God, but that God is bigger than the circumstances.

- We should set focused time to pray to the Lord once or twice a day either in a group or by ourselves.

- It can be seen as an interruption of your day, but it's not really disrupting your day to remind yourself that you belong to God.

📖 5
page 48
Outline Point B, 3

Empowerment

- We are not trying to increase our own personal influence and profile or the organization's influence and profile on the backs of those we claim to serve.

- Instead of seeking to increase our personal profile, we work to empower others.

- Our ministry partners are the heroes. That's why we feature them and not World Impact staff in World Impact videos. We want people to see our partners empowered to do the work of the Lord.

📖 6
page 49
Outline Point B, 4

Church Calendar

- Instead of viewing time only chronologically, we sanctify time by connecting our story to the story of God through the Church Year Calendar.

- This is a Christ-oriented way of understanding every day.

- Using the Church Year Calendar helps us to remember that, regardless of what may be happening in our lives and our hearts chronologically, we want to remember God's story by attaching our personal lives, our personal ministry to the story of God.

📖 7
page 49
Outline Point B, 5

Sabbath

- Instead of constant advocacy, we follow a pattern of work and rest.
- This is often violated amongst people who do ministry in communities of poverty.

📖 8
page 50
Outline Point B, 6

Personal Retreat

- Instead of a life of busyness and distraction, we take time to orient our lives towards obedience to God.
- Suggestion: take a workday once a month to reflect on your life, reflect on your work, look back at what's happened in the last month and plan for the coming month.

📖 9
page 50
Outline Point B, 7

Tithing

- Instead of anxiety about money, or worship of money, we generously give.
- Figure out what you should be giving and give it away to entities that help the economically poor.
- Make it a part of your own personal discipline to give of your own resources to the work of the Lord.

📖 **10**
page 51
Outline Point B, 8

Fasting

- Instead of seeking control, we fast in response to situations in life.

- Fasting from a biblical perspective is to get closer to God. And because you are closer to God, no matter what happens you will be able to handle it.

- It has to be disciplined within the framework of your own health.

📖 **11**
page 51
Conclusion

If you do all or most of the disciplines, it is impossible to ignore God. You can't get too far away from God if you are constantly doing things to remind yourself that you are supposed to be connected to God.

These are the eight disciplines that the Great Tradition (which all TUMI materials are based upon) displays.

📖 **12**
page 52
Student Questions and Response

Now allow the students to comment on what was presented. Here are some topics that can be discussed if you need to get the discussion going. (NOTE: Don't feel obligated to use them. If your class is going along well, allow the students to discuss freely.)

- Ask the class how they have been challenged to have personal time/vacation.

- Ask the class about their own physical habits of care: do they get enough sleep, are they eating well, are they exercising, are they drinking enough water, etc.?

- It was suggested to a group of community pastors who lived in a house in the neighborhood that they put a sign on the door: "Closed on Mondays" because they were constantly (daily, hourly) being asked for something. They thought the idea was demonic and unlike Jesus. You will actually teach them what your boundaries are, and they might, in return, actually learn some boundaries as well.

- After fourteen years as missionaries where people were always asking for something (every hour, hundreds of people being cared for by two), one of the two missionaries was having physical symptoms that were diagnosed as stress. They found out that vacations and retreats are very important.

- Or use the following discussion questions:

    1. Why is it important that advocacy is grounded in spiritual practices?

    2. In what practical ways have you tied your advocacy to your faith?

    3. How many of the spiritual practices do you engage in on a regular basis?

📖 13
page 53
Case Study

Discuss the Case Study:

You do poverty work in an urban neighborhood and run into a colleague at the corner store. He asks if you have some time to spare to talk. After walking to his office and starting to talk, it is apparent he is angry and frustrated. He is overwhelmed by the challenges he faces daily. The challenges don't shock you because you face the same ones. However, what does shock you is his tone and what he is saying. He is very cynical about the people in the neighborhood and the organizations set up to help them, including the local church he belongs to which he has stopped attending. His complaints revolve around not being appreciated for the sacrifices he has made and how physically tired he is. What would you tell him?

Let the students respond to this, but here are some suggested items to start off with:

- Allow him to vent and air out his issues. Then suggest that he can get some time off to spend time with the Lord. He seems to be disconnected from God.

- Encourage him to get back to fellowship in a church.
- One of the easiest things to do in ministry, especially if you're in a pastoral or supervisory role, is to think that you don't need a pastor.

📖 **14**
page 54
Other Assignments

Quizzes and answer keys for each lesson can be found online at World Impact U in the Redemptive Poverty Work Dashboard. (These are available to the Partner and Mentor.)

- Quiz 1: Lesson 1: A Brief Theological Reflection
- Quiz 2: Lesson 2: Toxic Poverty Work
- Quiz 3: Lesson 3: Redemptive Poverty Work
- Final Exam (includes questions from Lesson 4: Rhythms of Life and Poverty Work)
- Answer Key

After your students complete the Final Exam, please direct them to the *Redemptive Poverty Work Course Survey*. While we prefer this form be completed online, circumstances may prevent this from being possible. The form is included in the Appendix section of this book. Please scan the completed forms and send to the *Redemptive Poverty Work* representative.

- *Redemptive Poverty Work Course Survey* URL: https://tinyurl.com/d34tmhkv
- *Redemptive Poverty Work Course Survey* (see Appendix)

Appendix

Appendix 1: Course Schedule for *Redemptive Poverty Work*

Following is a sample of the course schedule for *Redemptive Poverty Work*. Find an editable version on the World Impact U *Redemptive Poverty Work* dashboard. Edit the details for your class and distribute to your students.

Appendix 2: *Redemptive Poverty Work* Course Survey

While we prefer this form to be completed online, circumstances may prevent this from being possible. Please scan the completed forms and send to the *Redemptive Poverty Work* representative.

APPENDIX / 41

APPENDIX 1
Course Schedule for *Redemptive Poverty Work*
Season, Year (ex. Fall 2021)
Name of Instructor
Date Range of the Class (ex. Nov. 17 - Dec. 22, 2021)

Meeting Information	Lesson and Assignments
Orientation Session *Face-to-Face Meeting* Date Time	***Orientation Session: Course Introduction*** Participate in Face-to-Face Meeting for Course Introduction

Session 1
 	
Face-to-Face Meeting
Date
Time
	Lesson 1, A Brief Theological Reflection
	Students should complete the following before this meeting:
	1. Complete Lesson 1 of *Redemptive Poverty Work* in the Student Workbook.
	2. Review questions at the end of the *Content* section of Lesson 1. Be prepared to discuss your answers in our Lesson 1 Face-to-Face Meeting.
	3. Complete the assignments in the *Assignments Due* section for Lesson 1 **before** our Lesson 1 Face-to-Face Meeting. Those assignments are as follows:
	  a. Read the following in *Redemptive Poverty Work*:
	    • *Introduction (pages 11-15)*
	    • *A Brief Theological Reflection (pages 17-22)*
	  b. Read the following in *Uncommon Church*:
	    • *Foreword* by Efrem Smith
	    • Chapter 3: *Jesus Did, Not Jesus Would: Jesus and the Condition of Poverty*
	    • Chapter 6: *Faith and Works: Eliminating the Tension between Evangelism and Justice*
	  c. Complete your summary of the readings on the *Reading Completion Sheet* for each reading listed above.
	  d. **Memorize Matthew 25.45** and grade yourself using the *Scripture Memory Grading Form*.
	After Face-to-Face Meeting:
	  Take the Lesson 1 Quiz.

Meeting Information	Lesson and Assignments
Session 2	**Lesson 2, Toxic Poverty Work**

Face-to-Face Meeting
Date
Time
	Students should complete the following before this meeting:
	1. Complete Lesson 2 of *Redemptive Poverty Work* in the Student Workbook.
	2. Review questions at the end of the *Content* section of Lesson 2. Be prepared to discuss your answers in our Lesson 2 Face-to-Face Meeting.
	3. Complete the assignments in the *Assignments Due* section for Lesson 2 **before** our Lesson 2 Face-to-Face Meeting. Those assignments are as follows:
	   a. Read the following in *Redemptive Poverty Work*:
	      • *Toxic Poverty Work (pages 23-30)*
	   b. Read the following in *Uncommon Church*:
	      • Chapter 2: *What Would Jesus Do? Poverty Is a Condition, Not an Identity*
	      • Chapter 7: *There Goes the Neighborhood: Understanding the Powers That Be*
	   c. Complete your summary of the readings on the *Reading Completion Sheet* for each reading listed above.
	   d. **Memorize Luke 4.18-19** and grade yourself using the *Scripture Memory Grading Form*.
	After Face-to-Face Meeting:
	Take the Lesson 2 Quiz.

Meeting Information	Lesson and Assignments
Session 3 *Face-to-Face Meeting* 　Date 　Time	**Lesson 3, Redemptive Poverty Work** *Students should complete the following before this meeting:* 1. Complete Lesson 3 of *Redemptive Poverty Work* in the Student Workbook. 2. Review questions at the end of the *Content* section of Lesson 3. Be prepared to discuss your answers in our Lesson 3 Face-to-Face Meeting. 3. Complete the assignments in the *Assignments Due* section for Lesson 3 **before** our Lesson 3 Face-to-Face Meeting. Those assignments are as follows: 　a. Read the following in *Redemptive Poverty Work*: 　　• Redemptive Poverty Work (pages 31-36) 　b. Read the following in *Uncommon Church*: 　　• Chapter 4: *The People of God: God's Plan for a Broken World* 　　• Chapter 8: *Championing the Community: Empowering Grassroots Leaders and Workers* 　　• Chapter 10: *The Kingdom Is in Us* 　c. Complete your summary of the readings on the *Reading Completion Sheet* for each reading listed above. 　d. **Memorize John 1.14** and grade yourself using the *Scripture Memory Grading Form*. *After Face-to-Face Meeting:* Take the Lesson 3 Quiz.

Meeting Information	Lesson and Assignments

Session 4
 	
Face-to-Face Meeting
Date
Time
	Lesson 4, Rhythms of Life and Poverty Work
	
	Students should complete the following before this meeting:
	
	1. Complete Lesson 4 of *Redemptive Poverty Work* in the Student Workbook.
	
	2. Review questions at the end of the *Content* section of Lesson 4. Be prepared to discuss your answers in our Lesson 4 Face-to-Face Meeting.
	
	3. Complete the assignments in the *Assignments Due* section for Lesson 4 **before** our Lesson 4 Face-to-Face Meeting. Those assignments are as follows:
	   a. Read the following in *Redemptive Poverty Work*:
	      • *Rhythms of Life and Poverty Work (pages 37-50)*
	   b. Read the following in *Uncommon Church*:
	      • Chapter 1: *Advocacy Is Not Enough*
	      • Chapter 5: *Doing Healthy Church: Seven Habits Toward Spiritual Maturity*
	      • Chapter 9: *Chasing Wild Dreams: Examples of Faith, Hope, and Love in Action*
	   c. Complete your summary of the readings on the *Reading Completion Sheet* for each reading listed above.
	   d. **Memorize Acts 2.42** and grade yourself using the *Scripture Memory Grading Form*.
	
	After Face-to-Face Meeting:
	   a. Take the Final Exam.
	   b. Complete the Course Evaluation Form.

Date	**Final Assignments Due** 1. Final Exam 2. Redemptive Poverty Work Course Evaluation Form

APPENDIX 2
Redemptive Poverty Work **Course Survey**

We greatly value your input and are here to serve you! Please answer the following Questions to give feedback on the training you received and who you are. The better we understand who you are and what you need, the better we can craft our resources and programs for your benefit.

1. Church, Ministry Network, or Organization

    What is the name of the organization that hosted this course?

2. How likely are you to recommend this course to a close peer or colleague? Please select 1-5

    5 = Definitely would recommend

    4 = Probably would recommend

    3 = Might recommend

    2 = Probably would not recommend

    1 = Would not recommend

Please answer questions 3, 4, and 5 based on the following rating scale:

   5 = Exceeded my expectations

   4 = Slightly above my expectations

   3 = Met my expectations

   2 = Slightly below my expectations

   1 = Did not meet my expectations

3. How would you rate the content in the course you just completed? (rate on scale of 1-5) _____

    Would you like to comment on your "course content" rating?

4. How would you rate your instructor (rate on scale of 1-5)? _____

   Would you like to comment on your instructor's rating?

5. Overall, did the course meet your expectations (rate on scale of 1-5)? _____

   Would you like to comment on your "course expectations" rating?

6. How might we improve this learning experience?

7. Name of the Instructor for this course:
   (Please DO NOT enter your name here.)

   _____   _____
   First Name   Last Name

   Email address of your instructor: _____

The instructor will receive a report on their ratings anonymously. All names and detailed information will not be shared with them.

Personal Information

None of this data will be shared with your personal information attached. This is simply for data collection.

First Name:

Last Name:

Email Address:

Are you currently incarcerated (please circle one)? Yes / No

Sex/Gender (please circle one): Male / Female

Ethnicity (please select one of the following):

    a. Asian/Pacific Islander

    b. Bi-racial, Multi-racial

    c. Black

    d. Latino

    e. Native American

    f. White

Birth Year (e.g., 1976): _____

Thank you for completing this survey!

www.ingramcontent.com/pod-product-compliance
Lightning Source LLC
Chambersburg PA
CBHW080403250426
43667CB00052B/2910